More Praise for Inside the Money Machine

"This is gritty new work by one of North America's best poets.
Each poem reveals the sweat and labor of the many who are trying
to get by in this tough, new world where big corporations and
Wall Street are sucking all of our humanity dry. These poems are
the voices of ourselves crying out." —M.L. LIEBLER, poet and editor
of *Working Words: Punching the Clock & Kicking Out the Jams*

"Minnie Bruce Pratt peels away at capitalism, 'the money machine,'
which is also the war machine. *Inside the Money Machine* is stun-
ning anti-capitalist poetics in action." —DON MEE CHOI, author
of *The Morning News Is Exciting*

"Minnie Bruce Pratt's poetry possesses an eloquent yet inflamed
indignation. The narratives in *Inside the Money Machine* are as
devastating for their language as for the stories they tell of the
vulnerable and disenfranchised among us. We see laid-off workers
huddle, 'staggered by catastrophe,' and rail riders jostled toward
hope, 'funneled into/the city terminal,…step down into the white
light of next…' Her poems ignite both longing and rage."
—MINDY KRONENBERG, Editor, *Book/Mark Quarterly Review*

Also by Minnie Bruce Pratt

THE DIRT SHE ATE: SELECTED AND NEW POEMS

WALKING BACK UP DEPOT STREET

S/HE

REBELLION: ESSAYS 1980–1991

CRIME AGAINST NATURE

WE SAY WE LOVE EACH OTHER

THE SOUND OF ONE FORK

YOURS IN STRUGGLE: THREE FEMINIST PERSPECTIVES
ON ANTI-SEMITISM AND RACISM, co-authored with
Elly Bulkin and Barbara Smith

FEMINISM AND WAR: CONFRONTING U.S. IMPERIALISM,
co-edited with Chandra Talpade Mohanty and
Robin Lee Reilly

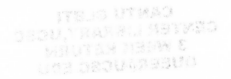

Inside the Money Machine

Inside the Money Machine

To Deb

To respect and solidarity in the struggle

Minnie Bruce

Minnie Bruce Pratt

6/11

Poetry Series #13

CAROLINA WREN PRESS
Durham, North Carolina

Series Editor: Andrea Selch

Design: Lesley Landis Designs
Cover Image: "roses in the West Village @ night" © 2009 Leslie Feinberg
Author Photograph: Leslie Feinberg

*The mission of Carolina Wren Press is to seek out, nurture and
promote literary work by new and underrepresented writers,
including women and writers of color.*

Carolina Wren Press is a 501(c)3 non-profit organization supported
in part by grants and generous individual donors. In addition, we
gratefully acknowledge the ongoing support of Carolina Wren
Press's activities made possible through gifts to the Durham Arts
Council's United Arts Fund. Special thanks to the North Carolina
Arts Council for a grant supporting this publication.

Library of Congress Cataloging-in-Publication Data

Pratt, Minnie Bruce.
Inside the money machine / Minnie Bruce Pratt.
    p. cm. -- (Poetry series ; #13)
ISBN 978-0-932112-60-6
ISBN 978-0-932112-02-6 (PDF eBook)
ISBN 978-0-932112-65-1 (ePub eBook)
I. Title.

PS3566.R35I57 2011
811'.54--dc22

2010040538

"The only danger is not going far enough."

—*Muriel Rukeyser*

FOR MILT NEIDENBERG

mentor, labor organizer, comrade, friend

Table of Contents

ARE YOU READY, WILLING, ABLE TO WORK?

All That Work No One Knows / 1

Breakfast / 2

Making a Phone Call / 3

Getting Money at the ATM / 5

Drinking Coffee / 6

Mailing a Letter / 8

Opening the Mail / 9

Making Art / 10

Walking Home from Work / 11

Washing Clothes / 12

Driving a Subway Train / 13

Giving a Manicure / 14

Cutting Hair / 15

Farming in the City / 16

A Small Business / 17

Ordering Paperclips / 18

Going Out of Business / 19

Going to Buy a Newspaper / 20

Getting a Pink Slip / 21

Laid Off / 22

The Unemployment Office / 23

Looking for Work / 24

Chopping Peppers / 25

FOR EVERY DREAM THERE'S A JACKPOT

Playing the Lottery   /   29

Making Another Phone Call   /   30

Reading the Classifieds   /   31

Shopping for a Present   /   32

Painting the Hall   /   33

Picking Up a Job Application   /   34

Selling a Brand   /   35

Selling Women   /   36

Forgetting to Clock Out   /   37

Collecting Social Security   /   38

Retirement   /   39

Waking to Work   /   40

ENOUGH!

Driving to a New Job   /   43

Driving to Work Again   /   44

Eating Alone   /   45

Writing Poetry in a Rented Kitchen   /   46

A Temporary Job   /   47

Beating the Heat   /   48

Driving the Bus after the Anti-War March   /   49

Riding the Trailways into the City   /   50

Playing the Guitar Underground   /   51

Breakfast Again   /   52

Hooking Up the Power   /   54

Teaching a Child to Talk   /   55

Shoveling Sand   /   56

Picketing the Bargain Store   /   57

Passing Food Up and Down the Table   /   58

Demanding Water   /   59

Ants, Massing   /   60

IF WE JUMP UP NOW

Fighting Fire   /   63

Distribution   /   64

Standing in the Elevator   /   66

Flight   /   67

The New Commuter War   /   68

Tegucigalpa   /   69

Sparks Fly Upwards   /   70

Arwhoolie   /   71

A Pile of Dirt at the Museum   /   72

Opening the Book on Tomorrow   /   73

Answering the Automated Voice   /   74

The Street of Broken Dreams   /   75

The Dow Turns Red   /   76

The Wednesday after May Day   /   77

The Great Leafing-Out   /   78

Burning Water   /   79

If We Jump Up   /   81

Notes   /   82

Acknowledgements   /   84

ARE YOU READY
WILLING
ABLE TO WORK?

All That Work No One Knows

We're not machines, you know. There's only so much we can take,
always more than we can, until we can't. Today I hold the weight
low in my belly and back, guts coiled tight from work at my desk.
Flat on the mat at the gym, I pull my legs open, my hipbones press
down like knives, slicing pain, my estranged being hiding out down
there. Knees up, rocking side to side, the pendulum rhythm, time
inside me, belly clock, basket of bone. What else have I carried?

Two babies, rattling inside a shaking gourd, little fish in a reed creel.
Each I hauled, both of us, around for months, like an oak-splint
laundry basket hiked in front of me with both hands, steady balance
until I could pull out the heavy wet baby and hold it up to dry.
All that work no one knew about but me. I wove sinew, vein, artery,
eyes and hair. Night and day. All that work no one knew about but me.

I was down south when I carried them. Later I came up north to learn
these cities, these other rivers, the work at the long eddy and curve
where rafts of timber waited to float down at Basket-Switch,
where the railroad finally came to pick up blue flagstones piled high
at the dock, the men who mined the mountain ribs by hand and chisel,
the women packing apples into barrels, into baskets, into wooden lugs,
a thousand trainloads from orchards they tended that finally rotted
to the ground, the people gone, the words between gone to the air.

What's left now are pyramids of fruit piled up in supermarkets,
a few saleable kinds, the red of Jonathan, Cortland, Sweet Winesap,
and the grass giving way to other trees, the valley down river
flowing dense as midnight even in mid-day, growing dark again.

Somewhere, further west, a first woman weaves her Delaware
basket again. Somewhere a basket is brought to her grave
and the weave torn through, or her last pot brought and broken,
so all her life of work runs out, down and back into the ground,
past her head and her hands, her belly, her feet, to where it came.
The fumbled load we carry, the jumble, our lives unknown,
we who make and are shaped, we who hold and are held.

Breakfast

Rush hour, and the short-order cooks lob breakfast
sandwiches, silverfoil softballs, up and down the line.
We stand until someone says, *Yes?* The next person behind
breathes hungrily. The cashier's hands never stop. He shouts:
Where's my double double? We help. We eliminate all verbs.
The superfluous *want, need, give* they already know. Nothing's left
but *stay* or *go*, and a few things like *bread*. No one can stay long,
not even the brown stolid man in blue-hooded sweats, head down, eating,
his work boots powdered with cement dust like snow that never melts.

Making a Phone Call

She says her name is Daisy but it's really Meena,
and I'm in New Jersey and she's in Delhi or Mumbai.
Or I'm in Alabama and she's in Albuquerque inside
sand-tinted concrete that blends in with the desert.
One room, one-thousand three-hundred-fifty people,
mostly women, each sitting in her place, the one chair,
a desk with stuffed animals, a flag, a photo frame open
like a book to show off the children, easy to pack up
when they lay her off. But, any day now, her green vine
creeping along the divider will reach the window if
sales are good, if she's lucky. Outside, desert. Beyond,
the blue mountains. Eight-and-a-half hours a day, minus
ten minutes, minus thirty, minus ten, for breaks and lunch.
She takes orders for clothes, she checks on my mother's
health insurance, she doesn't make a thing, it's a service,
not the steel mill blasting production, the slag, coal, ore, fire,
twenty thousand people, mostly men, two-story machines.
But Milt says: *If she works on anything, touches anywhere,
she creates the wealth of the world. What comes back to her?*

Today my one conversation is Rhonda, office supplies,
she says the truck is on the way, traffic on the Turnpike.
How does she know? The radio? Satellite tracking the driver?
I tell her I can see out my front window the trucks and cars
backed up, the waiting line to enter the Tunnel, the traffic
a metal wall around the city. Needing to talk to someone.
Everyone stuck for hours, cell phones scorching their ears.

The call centers, now they make them like assembly lines,
they say leave your mind at home, tighten the bolt. But no one
stops thinking. We think all the time: *Why am I doing this?*
The college fund or the rent, but it isn't the money, really,
she says, the best part is the people, you're with them all day,
you get to know them, you forget sometimes you're doing it
for someone else. She has to stand up if she wants to see
another person, her braid swings, she pulls her sari past

the blinking blue screen, next thing she knows, the chairs
are gone, the cubicles are being broken down and stacked,
to be sent elsewhere, turn-key ready for cheaper wages, while
money pours in electronic waves through satellite dishes, back
to the company from fifty-plus countries where it does business.

She opens her desk drawer, she takes out her keys and her folding altar,
something to hold in her hand as she and the other women walk out
    the door,
in her palm, small as a notepad, Saraswati, Lakshmi, Shakti,
    wisdom, wealth, the source.

Getting Money at the ATM

I can hear someone behind the money machine, a muffled
clanking. The screen blinks and promises me *any time,*
any where. A secret password gets me twenty dollars right
in the palm of my hand, dispensed quick as candy. And
not flimsy paper worn down like knee pads in work jeans,
but crisp new money fronted by old faces, by big men
who promise a pyramid of power, an all-seeing eye, every
thing is mine if I hold this magic skin mottled and blotched
with strange letters and numbers. Cash from last month's
paycheck, from electronic pulses, from the hidden vault.

From me sitting at my desk last month, phone to my ear,
words trembling on my tympanum, ten thousand words
pounding on the membrane, how many thousand clacking
between my teeth and tongue, the hyoid bone, the mandible
working without being named, that many thousand words
spoken by my fingers on the keyboard. Twelve eye muscles
twisting to follow the serpentine light of the screen. Feet
pushing the swivel chair back and forth, printer, phone, fax
machine. Taking a break means walking down four flights,
ten minutes up the street to the bank, then the quickie mart.
At the counter I hand over money, a paper token, a one-page
book, all my comings and goings hidden in it, mystified.

So, it's farewell and go, little book, and who will handle my life next,
and not know it? Then, it's back. Back up the stairs. Sit at my desk.

Drinking Coffee

At the Journal Square Deli, a stocky short grey-haired white woman wearing blue ear muffs, not much older than me, rather mannish, comes up to me while I'm sitting at the table, and says, in a flat high-pitched voice, *Will you buy me an orange juice?* I look up, bewildered. *Will you buy me an orange juice? I'll be sitting over here.* And sits down two tables away, a small single table. A white man with a cane behind me laughs, cane laid across the top of his table, and says, *She wants you to buy an orange juice and give it to her.* I say, *I know,* and get out my wallet, two dollar bills, and walk over to her, press them into her hand. *Here, you can get it for yourself.* But she says, plaintively, also a little bit bewildered, *Where is it? How much is it? They won't sell it to me, they won't let me sit here.* So I go to the case and get "pure premium" juice, a pint, pay for it, and get 65 cents in change, and take it to her, put the carton in her hands and the change on the table. She says, *Thank you.* I say, *You're welcome,* and sit back down. One of the staff, a skinny Latino maybe not older than high school, is mopping the floor around our feet. She says, again in that flat high voice, *Hi! Hi! Do you like your job?* He says something very low that I can't hear, and mops away without pausing. She drink her juice, and walks to the side door, pausing to throw out her carton and say to the two older burly white men in winter coats sitting nearby, *Hi! Hi!* One is wearing a pair of Nike sneakers without socks. Outside the wind chill is 15 degrees. She goes out into the concourse and walks a few steps, stops, hesitates as if she's forgotten, as if she's remembered something, then walks slowly on.

Upstairs, in the long line at the bank, an African-American woman with a just-walking child is anxiously looking through her purse, *I guess it's not here, not here, wait a minute, baby.* An East Indian man in his sixties is nervously aligning the checks in his hand. A white man in jeans calls out to the tellers: *Could you speed this up?* Out in the foyer a Latina is saying to her friend, looking in her purse, *I thought I had $20 left in here, I had $100 at the start of the day.* She enumerates each purchase and bill she paid during the day.

At the Starbucks on the Gold Coast by the river, two white men in suits bend their heads together over their cappuccinos, antiphony, alternating whisper and louder. One says: *Thirty million dollars…increasing value….* The other parries: *The company was for sale. The stock price went up but….* One lowers his voice: *And it's illegal to…the net unrealized earnings…1.7 million now but….* The other laughs: *They don't fire people who are….* He laughs again: *They fire people who….*

Sometimes I go by the money machine at Fleet Bank when I walk to get coffee; there's a branch above the Deli and another by the Starbucks. The drivers for armored trucks are told to hit the accelerator between their stops to pick up cash, speed up, speed up. No time for a coffee break. The time while the money sits alone in the truck is time when no one is making money on it.

Mailing a Letter

Through the double-thick pane of plastic glass, we talk.
Time for two, three sentences, no more, as the line lengthens.
To others, Marguerita says, *Qué pasa?* When I ask, Lisa just
smiles. Atul says, *My feet, my back.* Sometimes as he sorts
the morning delivery through the lozenge of my open mailbox,
I see his mouth. He says, *It's OK, I can talk. My hand is working.*

As they talk, their hands punch, check, stamp, write names
in triplicate. They take and give money. They bundle our letters.
The walls are piled with boxes of our words, folded, sealed,
ready to travel far beyond us. The relation between us becomes
the relation between things, and words turn into numbers.

My letter, like every place on earth, has its denomination,
and so Mr. A. punches it in. He has the book of codes,
but perhaps he still worries. In Gujarat the earthquake folds up
houses until no one is left to write home to. Perhaps he worries
like my neighbor, Mr. Goldstein, who carried dead letters home
from work. At night he searched his atlas for the scrawled lost
cities, places someone was trying to get back to, places someone
had never been. When they carried him out, I was in the foyer,
getting my mail out of the metal grille of boxes. He was a lump
under a sheet on a stretcher. For days he was a sweet stench
at the door of his apartment, his one room, the walls stacked
chin-high with neatly tied bundles of letters, and on his desk
a little pile of letters. Some he had opened. The others, not.

Opening the Mail

She used to work down in the copy center, and,
don't get her wrong, she liked it, she did. The big
xerox engines purred, paper rolled out like money
and shot into slots like a casino payoff. But this job,
there's something new every day, the letters come in,
hundreds, thousands, from all over the place, and she
gets to open every one. The message in a bottle, the note
slid into the cashier's cage, the letter left on the bed
when she walked out the door, the handkerchief dropped
behind him during the game at recess. She slices each
open with her knife, logs it and routes it to the *other girls*.

But her dream is to get a camper and follow the NASCAR
races. Six days travel and on Sunday stand inside the final
circuit of sound, inside that belly. It's not the same as on TV
where it seems like they are just going round and round. Not
the same at all, she says. Every moment counts, and the air
smells like burning oil. Any minute it could burst into flames.

Making Art

Tom went home to Old Shotts where his uncle said,
with satisfaction, they were getting rid of the pit bings,
all of them. The slag heaps, he'd watched the night train
labor up their scalene sides to dump orange fire, molten
stone, burning its impure shape into his memory's eye.
After school he'd caught the work bus home, and the men,
black-clad and fearsome, hung on its side and shouted,
come up out of the ground alive. Their steaming breath,
the train's exhaust, all that's left are the bings, somewhere
near Glasgow, beautiful to him as the pyramids in Egypt.

When I first moved to this city and took a train through
the fractured rock, I saw someone had made the walls
into art bolted with bronzed green screws, with red rust,
with circled squares outlined in blue, draped in lush mesh,
steel netting to catch corroded stone as it falls, scattered
fluorescent numbers, meaningful marks. All unknown
to me when I stood, a child in the dark, looking fifty miles
north at the pink glow smearing the night sky. Something
huge making that fire beyond the horizon, beyond my ken.

Walking Home from Work

The man in a suit and his dog in harness stand at the corner.
The eyes of people getting off the bus flick at him, flick away.
The light blinks yellow and I step into a lull, a space between cars,
walking away from noise. Half a block, then behind me a clink,
a jingle, coins in a pocket or a can being kicked by the wind.

I turn and it's the man I'd forgotten since I thought I would outpace him.
On I walk until my shoes crunch gravel by the new construction.
Now the sound I make is only one in a thousand. Now I am no more
than an echo location, a mark in the air, a noise he might use to fathom
his way from here to the next corner, walking home with his dog
    from work.

Washing Clothes

At the laundromat, under cracked glass, a one-page flier
for yoga. Blue letters on white paper. Blue sky, white clouds.
The classes are upstairs, above the machines that turn and hum
and turn like giant clocks counting out each minute of each hour.

A woman who works at the laundromat, a Puertoriqueña,
slings heavy wet clothes like small corpses out of, into, machines,
later gathering them to her, warm and revived. In between times,
she reads some poems, they're just the right length, while
the tumblers click, a calculator adding up her wages by the hour.

Driving a Subway Train

It's Monday and, nail polish off, carhart jacket on, he's left behind
the clothes that fit her secret self, the weekend self people know.
Five days a week he moves toward home under ground, he sits
in the cab, hunched over, and smokes. The cigarette's red tip points
at the moving dark in the tunnel, the steel rails, hypnotic labyrinth,
go, amber slow, stop. Then under the river full throttle to the white-lit
ledges, Ninth St., Christopher, people perched to step into their cages.
He bids on the rush-hour shift so he can shotgun the train through
its channel, a whistle, the blast of daylight at the end. The ground
spits him out near the yellow bouffant skirts of forsythia, or later,
on his way home, as pink flower confetti tumble idly on the street,
he watches the wind turning petals into tiny cyclones at her feet.

Giving a Manicure

The woman across from me looks so familiar,
but when I turn, her look glances off. At the last
subway stop, we rise. I know her, she gives manicures
at Flower Nails. She has held my hands between hers
several times. She nods and smiles. There the women
wear white smocks like technicians, and plastic tags
with their Christian names. Susan? No, not Susan,
whose hair is cropped short, who is short and stocky.
Sylvia, this older lady who does hands while music,
often Mozart, plays. People passing by outside are
doubled in the wall mirror. Two of everyone walk
forward, backward, vanish at the edge of the shop.
Susan does pedicures—pumice on heels, bends over,
kneads feet in the water like laundry. She pounds
calves with her fists and her cupped palms slap
a working beat, *p'ansori* style. She talks to the others
without turning her head, a call in a language shouted
hoarse across fields where a swallow flew and flew
across the ocean, and then fetched back to Korea
a magic gourd seed, back to the farmer's empty house
where the seed flew from its beak to sprout a green vine.
When the farmer's wife cut open the ripe fruit, out spilled
seeds of gold. Choi Don Mee writes that some girls
in that country crush petals on their nails, at each tip
red flowers unfold. Yi Yon-ju writes that some women
there, as here, dream of blades, knives, a bowl of blood.

Cutting Hair

She pays attention to the hair, not her fingers, and cuts herself
once or twice a day. Doesn't notice anymore, just if the blood
starts flowing. Says, *Excuse me* to the customer and walks away
for a band-aid. Same spot on the middle finger over and over,
raised like a callus. Also the nicks where she snips between
her fingers, the torn webbing. Also spider veins on her legs now,
so ugly, though she sits in a chair for half each cut, rolls around
from side to side. At night in the winter she sleeps in white
cotton gloves, neosporin on the cuts, vitamin E, then heavy
lotion. All night, for weeks, her white hands lie clothed like
those of a young girl going to her first party. Sleeping alone,
she opens and closes her long scissors and the hair falls under
her hands. It's a good living, kind of like an undertaker,
the people keep coming, and the hair, shoulder length, french
twist, braids. Someone has to cut it. At the end she whisks
and talcums my neck. Only then can I bend and see my hair,
how it covers the floor, curls and clippings of brown and silver,
how it shines like a field of scythed hay beneath her feet.

Farming in the City

Going downhill, Newark Avenue, I stand at the graveyard fence
where dried-up brown grass smells like hay did in the old barn,
big rectangles piled up, just a few against the back of the loft,
enough for one cow and one mule, last of the farm's withering.

The gravestones are cut uphill by Pompilio and Sons, *scalpellini*,
in a little empty shop where some days a man comes in to carve
the name that's been called. Waiting for him, the stones sit blank,
glossy faces lined up on a tiny plot of grass. Selim said, first day
he looked down from his window, he almost left, seeing the dead.

Now he and the stonecutter talk at the back fence, their shared
language of the last century, Italia's foot in Egypt. Selim says:
We have our ways. He grows grapes on his trellis, and gives away
clusters of perfume, tough-skinned, to customers. His wife's mother
is from Salerno, the mountains. They farmed, they grew chestnuts.
Her father's last job was the cemetery, West Side, a gardener farming
on top of the bodies. In summer the *genena* behind Selim's store is cool.
The stone slab floor took four men to lift off the truck, heaving,
straining under a weight that promises to level them to the ground.

A Small Business

In the cold twilight, I walk and hear the beginning of spring,
the swamp frogs' high pitch, like crickets later in the year, but
it's the shimmy squeal of an idling car. At the mail-drop store
she says business is off, not much shipped at the holidays
this winter, but spring is coming, people will wear white
and play the old *Holi* game of throwing color in the streets,
each drenched in purple and pollen-powdered by pink. Then
summer, but in the islands the heat isn't like here, or the houses,
they open up at the top and back, so there's ventilation, a breeze.
And the dirt! She misses the dirt, that's why she can't live
in an apartment. But people here grow grass in their rooms.
She watches these TV shows, they tell you how. You plant
in disposable aluminum ovenware, and put it on a table. The fan
blows, the grass moves back and forth in the wind. Her hands
wave from side to side. You can put candles in it. One woman
said she put the pan of grass on the floor and stood in it,
    barefooted.

Ordering Paperclips

Two jobs ago I had an office, I could walk downstairs
to talk to someone, her office was like a hand-crafted
box inside old stone walls. Inside, it was quiet except
when she was making her calls. Her mother in the box
factory stood all day on dirt floors, folding, could
see daylight through the walls, and sometimes a snake
ran over her feet like a length of muscle or intestine
gone astray, and she finally quit, never the same after.

Then her father—Because of the layoffs, he had to
work a new machine, saw the pressure at red, pushed
the woman by him away. In the hospital he asked for
a knife to slice his second skin off. Outside her window
snow fell, students trampled the snow. After a while she
sat and ordered paperclips. The radiator hissed in her ear:
Fear is what keeps us in our jobs, until there is a bigger fear.

Going Out of Business

Time is running out for the Ames Discount Store,
and we know it, that's why we're here, roaming
back and forth, up and down the aisles, looking for
something we can afford in this tomb of things
made by someone else, somewhere else. I know.
Not long ago it was my mother pushed the cloth
into the needle's tooth, and when the machine bit,
blood stood like a red gem on her finger.

What will happen to all this stuff? More than we
can buy, but it's so sad to leave it behind, buried
here. The days and nights someone like me sat, cut,
glued, stapled, folded, hurried to finish one more piece.

Now it gleams, heaped up, waiting for someone to use.
But I have a budget. I pick up silver gift-wrap paper,
put it back. One man stands, jeans pressed, flannel shirt,
baseball cap. Hand in pocket, he stares at watches
under glass. Hundreds of eyes blink and look back.

We leave the store by ones and twos, most with nothing
but a white plastic bag tossing in our hands, almost empty, slack.

Going to Buy a Newspaper

Out the window, the street is fogged in,
a slope of pasture down toward the river.
Day after day, the buildings are there, brick-willed.

They meet the sun again, or shadow rain.
Then I walk by some morning and one is gone,
knocked down, no stronger than a person.

In the fast-food place, the old men sit by the window,
remember how good the sun feels on their shoulders, how
good, they'll never go to the old folks' building.

At the supermarket, the checkout clerk says, *The boss*
compares us with each other, adds up our tapes,
one morning either you or someone else is gone.

Getting a Pink Slip

Mine is electronic, item 13 in a memo, then the phone,
and then the legal letter from the school's president:
You'll be missed. He's mis-spelled my name.

I read the letter once and again. The words don't change.
When I tell people, either it's happened to them or it hasn't,
those inside the fence turning away, those of us outside in the line.

The pink slip in the pay envelope, the words that say you're laid off.
Fired. Out of there like a shell exploding from a howitzer. Canned
like tuna or corn, dead, done for, shipped out on the next truck.

Two women lean into each other, staggered by catastrophe,
the plant fence out of focus behind them. They hold up
a crumpled paper, like the photo of some beloved lost to murder
or to war, the evidence of what lived a few minutes before:
My job, my other self.

Laid Off

The security guard at Eddie Bauer's in the mall
doesn't know why it's closing. Not enough business,
maybe prices too high for people nowadays. The last
day? March 15, she knows that precisely, it's pinned
down. Everything must go. Customers in line shift
from foot to foot, dinner hour, hurry. The women
at the cash registers take their grim-faced time.
With the slowness of those laying out the dead,
they bag clothes with hands that no longer care.
I got the call yesterday. Thirty days. At a factory,
I might have gotten sixty, and re-training. And my
students? Always some piece of work left unfinished,
like a half-sewn sleeve.

The Unemployment Office

I stand in line with my friend until that is wrong.
The guard says punch in by phone, over there. The women
said, *Going to get my pennies,* and swung their handbags
down the aisle between machines. Ten million out of work.
Where are the others? More computers than people
in the room. The automated voice asks, *Are you ready,
willing, able to work?* Yes, 1, No, 2. Fear squats in my belly,
takes out its pinchers and sets to work. My throat chokes
on words, oh, oh, oh, the whistle that no longer blows
at 7 a.m. The first time, I had a tiny book all my own,
where I wrote down my search. The others are at home,
punching their phones, and the counselors are fired.
No machine can do my job, the torque of my words
in someone's ear, but I cost money, the benefits package,
subsistence, flesh. Still, I'm not dead labor yet, a profit edge
to be made, my tongue and brain at a low enough wage.

In the morning grey I used to hear the garbage men
gee and *haw* the truck they hung on, right and left,
the mule plowing the field that's now a flat sandy plain,
a windowless factory going on and on, without end,
inside 6000 women and men with bloody hands
kill the hogs and cut them up, can't stand the job
more than a year. In the morning, a giant mechanical
hand pushes out from the garbage truck, closes on the
can, dumps it, throws it down. One man at the controls,
he's warm and lodged. What about the other two men,
Black men who rode, arms up, staring out and leaning
      into the curve,
aloof, flattened to the side, two pillars holding up
      an invisible roof.

Looking for Work

I don't have a job yet, all right? You ask every time you call.
Jobs don't grow on trees. The way my pa walked through
Los Angeles, past palms crowned with rats' nests, on foot
in the land of cars. He'd been a chauffeur to the stars,
a coalminer, he'd made tires, he'd worked in every state but
two, and he could not find a job. The thigh piston lifts the knee,
drives the foot down into the ground. *How can this be?*
I say, fast breath, as I drop my application into the slot.

What did he like about work under ground? Was it the dark
or was it the breaking through? The dark line of connection,
the seam of ore, a sentence to be read by other miners and him.
It ran for miles, it never ends until the money men sit down
to squeeze the world in their hands. They can afford to wait
until diamonds are done. Meanwhile, we struggle in the sun,
like people lined up by the church, dressed go-to-meeting neat.
When I ask why—*Food,* says one man, turning away. Yes, I'm afraid
that could be me soon. They said they'd hire me back the next day,
at my pay ten years ago. But I still have some savings, and my pride.

Chopping Peppers

The slice across the top, at right angles, and
I am inside. If I did this for a job, where would I be?
Sitting on a milk crate in a restaurant kitchen. Who
would I be? Someone chopping green peppers for
a hundred daily specials. I hold the slippery bowl
and inside is the secret, an island of seeds, a palisade,
a reef, an outcropping of the future waiting for decay,
for the collapse of walls, for escape. Instead, I filigree
the flesh into odd bits of ribbon with the little paring knife,
the gesture effortless, no more than a minute, time to play
with these words, and my fingers and wrist don't feel a thing.

I was no metaphor when I fed a machine eight hours a day.
I was what came before words, my hands the spring,
setting metal jaws to shut, the same synapses to snap
together every second all day again and again
until what was being done could be named.

FOR EVERY DREAM
THERE'S A JACKPOT

Playing the Lottery

At the table two women stare down at their cards,
classic bingo, cool cash: *For every dream there's a
jackpot.* The cards gleam silver pastel fire. On the table
are gloves, an old toboggan cap, two smashed paper
bags, an orange plastic pill bottle. One woman folds
her sandwich foil in half. The other scrapes her card
with a nickel. *Nada.* Clicking the coin on the table
to clean it between boxes, as the numbers come up
silver and gold, each box a window, a hundred new
views. Or a door, behind each door a new car,
a luxury vacation, next month's rent. *No lo tengo.*
Click, click, as if the turning wheel on *The Wheel
of Fortune* is slowing down to reach its final destination,
after Vanna White dressed like a goddess has flung
out her hand to settle with fate. These women keep
their coats on, looking for something more than job,
table, tavern, bed, the chance of the numbers runner
who jogs past the corner, the casual lift of his hand
to grab the paper slip stuck high on the light pole.
One woman folds the scrap of foil again by four,
eight, sixteen, then drops it into her purse to save.
Every card needs just one more number to win.

Making Another Phone Call

She says her job is awful, awful, the hours,
some days nothing at all, then it's come in
at 11 a.m. or 9 p.m., then nothing again.
The money is bad, and it's so boring. Boring.
All she does is annoy people, calls them up
and annoys them. How does she get rid
of that thing standing between her and what
she wants? She says God may show her.
But how much more does she need to see?
Every day she pulls her chest open and looks
at a ruined life. The heart all bloody. What is
the name of the thing eating up her only life?
Except for waitressing, this is the longest job
she's ever held. Her husband reminded her
the other night, she says, the longest job.

Reading the Classifieds

At the next table an African-American woman bows her head
over a pile of newspapers, her hand slant to her mouth, then
to her ear, smoothing her temple, smoothing the pulse, fear.
Her fingers again to her forehead, then to her heartbeat hollow,
her blood marking time. She looks at the clock, touches her hair,
gets up and goes. Two days later, another woman there, the same
table, a Latina leaning forward into the paper, one hand with
a yellow marker, one hand at her forehead, a mirror gesture.
Her fingers pleating, smoothing, as her eyes scan down, over,
as her hand unseeing fumbles toward the brown bag lunch.
The other hand reaches to mark with a gleam the *data entry,*
benefits, the *experience a plus,* the *knowledge a must.*
Not yet the *no experience,* not yet the *home mailers, home*
workers, or *escort needed.* No faxes, no phone calls. She
gets up, bound for an overheated anteroom where she'll meet
herself, sitting on plastic stacking chairs, five, ten, twenty times
over. Next table a white man with shoes but no socks complains
about the cold, says, *This weather. This fucking*
weather. Reminds me of what I was, on the street.

Shopping for a Present

The cashier says, *Thirty-nine ninety-five.* Her infra-red eye
beams at a box the size of a bed pillow, back massager, promise
pain will end. Then the young man from his great guarded height
slowly extends a hand, unfurls fingers to show two crumpled twenties.
As if he doesn't recognize the faces twisted in his palm, as if
that's all he has in his pocket. The hand offering up its labor for
a device, a hope, someone else, the figure bending, sitting, standing,
lying down. *No relief,* she says to him at 4 a.m., leaning against
the kitchen counter as he pulls on his boots. To give her something
soft, cotton lamb's wool cover pulled around an appliance, boxed,
the shadow figures along the assembly line pushing it forward
toward him. Soft for what no hand, no touch as yet has mended.
His hand, extended, grasps the plastic bag straps and he walks out
as I pay and follow into the dark crowded street, the holiday hustle,
the hooded man silently holding up fliers for *Men's Suits, All Sizes,*
the charity kettle ringing for pennies and dimes some shoppers fling in.

Painting the Hall

We didn't know which door to knock on, front room or kitchen?
We had pink roses in our hands, the holiday basket, the super's
bonus, the green wish of money in an envelope: Thank-you
for the new locks, brass hands clasped across our door, and floor
tiles laid down smooth as new skin over a scrape. Thank-you for
light, the plugged-in neon eye. For the mesh screen, the grout,
the new ball-cock in the toilet, the rubber washer on the faucet.

When we finally knocked, there was a pause, a scrabbling.
Maria opened the door but didn't say ¡Papi! She led us through
the accordion rooms to his bed, where he staggered to stand.
We knew he'd been sick, back pain, could hardly walk. We
put the little basket by his hand. Thirty-eight years on the job,
and no health insurance. He'd cooked for some big company
the next town over. Later there was his daughter on the stairs
crying: *The doctor said if he'd just come in sooner, they could
have caught it.* The stairs, broken edges, smeared linoleum.
He painted the stairwell, four floors, perched on the ladder rungs
last winter, the hall up-slanting, bright-washed as beach sand.

Picking Up a Job Application

A spring wind hustles hundreds of pages into the street,
discarded leaflets like pieces of a shredded textbook
under the feet of high-school students let out for lunch.
A young woman bends and grasps a flier: sliver of promise,
passport to enter through the golden arches, gateway to the west,
up escalator to immediate opportunity, and prosperity somewhere
higher, those sky-reaching towers across the river looking down on her
and the crowd scrambling to buy a dollar-forty-nine-cent special meal.
Required? Just the have-a-nice-day sticker on her backpack,
the smiley face plastered over her eyes and nose and mouth every day.
And one thing more, of course: *Fill in application on the reverse—*
English only please. She speaks Hindi, Arabic, Tagalog, Wolof,
Greek, half a dozen other tongues hide behind her smiles. The day
she says *Hello* to her first customer is the day she says *Hello*
to the other women behind the counter, who are talking, but
    not smiling.

Selling a Brand

It's all written down in the Look Book, she says. That's a three-ring
binder bigger than her psych text. No uniforms, but black pants
or skirts, and girls have to wear pastel blouses, no blue, no purple,
no red. The guys can wear red, but only one earring, and only
in the right ear: *Well, you know, the left means you might be gay.*
The girls can do their nails, only in colors the store sells. If they put
their hair up, it has to be in a style, no ponytail. Why? *It's called
branding.* You walk into the store anywhere in the world, you look at
the staff, you know where you are. Sure, you can get fired if you don't,
like not shaving your legs, stockings over bare legs is the rule
if you wear a dress, but no hem above the knee. And no red, absolutely
no red, she says, blushing, no sex on sale: *That's over in lingerie.*

At the mall I refuse the perfumed spritz of young women wearing
black at the lip of the gaping store, but sometimes I go in to finger
the silky tissues, the membrane inside, something for a vacation
I'll never take, in a distant hot city I'll never visit. At the airport
coffee stand, I say, *No hurry, got your hands full,* to the woman
working the counter. The sidewalk slides behind me, moving people,
like items at a store checkout. She hands me a cup, says, *Busy, yeah.*
But not as bad as the donut shop, she had to quit, it was like a cult:
No jewelry, not even your wedding ring. They tell you what to wear
down to your underwear, so no one can see what's underneath.

Selling Women

On the cell phone to a friend, she says she was half-
naked, standing there crying in her bra and panties. He
banged on the door for eight minutes. *Eight!* She called
the police, then stared stark at the green phone screen,
the digital numbers that don't move, don't move.
Then he put his shoulder through the door and broke it
down. Silence. The jitney stops, people get on, off.
She makes another call, the landlord. Dead-ass serious,
some guy busting in, looking for a brothel: *Trying to fuck
me because of what you ran there back in the day.* This
is no joke, get real! Do something about the door.

Hanging by its hinges like a dislocated arm. Can't
stop anything from getting in. Summer night gun
metal grey, a storm coming, electric pulse stun,
and as we move up the street, flashes in the grass,
lightning bugs, little sparks floating up, fire-flakes.

Forgetting to Clock Out

On the last morning of getting up before dark
she drives to work and walks through the tunnel
pushing herself like a rattling empty gurney up
the long incline. She teaches her last class, pain
management, and tells the RNs: *Only the person in pain*
knows the level of pain. She stands in the empty room
afterwards, by the tangle of lift equipment, and looks
at how she set to work by age nine, cooking for family,
and then in the grapevines, clipping and coiling
the tendrils, tying up the green veins and arteries.
She is done with all that. She goes into her office,
and cleans out her desk. The company is keeping
her lessons plans, her reports on care innovation,
all the knowledge she made about the best way to take
the pulse, the breath, a step. A few women come by
and say, *Congratulations. We'll miss you.* Two
friends make her a plaque, *Working-Class Hero,*
because they remember the strike of 1983, how
the security guards fired from inside the hospital
on the nurses, how a car tried to ram through
their picket line. That's when she threw herself
onto the hood and stopped it. Even the doctors
remember that, but neither they nor anyone else
line the hallways as they should have in her honor,
when she leaves that afternoon at 5:15 p.m.,
        forgetting to clock out.

Collecting Social Security

Today I don't want to get old and live like Miss Brown.
The jaws of time are shutting, like elevator doors slam
on her slow caught arms. She's begun to walk up the stairs.
Breakfast is tea, cheese, a powdered donut. Supper, an egg
beaten into sherry. Counts eggs to the end of the month,
$690 a month to live on, and most of that goes to rent.
She asks: Why is it so easy for other people to die? Why
is it taking her so long? *God said honor thy father and mother*
that thy days may be long, but father died in the first war,
mother abandoned her. *Is this Thelma Brown who used to*
fly? Sixty years at the cash register, good for nothing now.

I'm here about the rent increase, the tenants' petition,
exempt the elderly. She wishes to be fair, would strive
to pay. *If He wants her to go on, He can help her, He's*
the one who made her. But she has something to show me.
When her last bird died, the mice came and took every bit
of him away. When the last bird died, she took a cab and
bought another. She got him for his blue breast, Alice blue,
they once had dresses that color. She couldn't see to walk,
can't, cataracts. Goes to the 7-11 with hands outstretched
and falls if her toe hits the curb. She thinks I'm like her.
If it's me, no others, no laughing in the hallway, she double-
unlocks the door. One room and a kitchen, boarded windows,
because the boys threw firecrackers that Fourth of July.

What she loves she keeps near her in a cage by the couch.
When she whistles, and lifts up the stained white towel,
I see a blue-and-white parakeet with its breast picked raw.

Retirement

She is still knitting even as her mind drops a stitch
every few seconds. She rips out rows of garbled yarn
in a fury. She says to her daughter: *I just want to die.*
She walks half a mile every morning outside the strip
mall, around the post office, the Dollar Store, the Rent-
A-Center. She puts on a shower cap and plastic apron
and serves up the food at the Senior Center. She says:
*I want to die. Not productive anymore. I sit here,
watching TV. Knitting, knitting, knitting.* To the ants
crawling on her kitchen counter, she says, *I am going to
kill you now,* just before she slaps down her hand.

Waking to Work

I wake, and in the moment before the next work begins,
a starling scrapes on the iron railing, a car horn blares
a line of known, aggravating rhythm: *Come. On. Come.*
On. Next to me, her skin to my skin, ground still warm
even as earth turns its face from the sun. Time going,
gone. In the hall the failing fire alarm chirps like a cricket.
On the subway a crumpled man slumps, head on his arm,
as one finger taps an almost motionless melody onto his knee.

How do we go on? Longing for something bigger than us.
But not this now, not this buying and selling. If we could each
make what we can, take what we need, and that be enough—

ENOUGH!

Driving to a New Job

Sure, I'm glad I have the job. Those rejection letters—
being told over and over: *No.* Or: *Sorry, not this time.*
I was an old tool hanging up on the side of an old
lean-to shed, metal curved like a wing, wood handle
lathed by all who touched, but no one around could
remember what I was used for. Then some friends
found me this job. I drive over the Endless Mountains,
up and back every week, about four hours, through
long slides of coal and iron country, slabs of grey-
rose rock exposed along the way. About four hours,
five if the weather's bad. The car fishtails in rain sluicing
off the hills. Say five. Time enough between Bartonsville
and Binghamton to finish one poem before I arrive.

Driving to Work Again

6:15 a.m. Grey cloud camouflage netting overhead. Bloodstains
develop on the horizon, slow as a polaroid exposure. The Thruway,
Wednesday, mid-week, so eighteen-wheelers are a rolling supply
chain, lit up like supermarkets. Once my travel was on foot, Sunday
afternoons, my aunt pointing to a root-home flung round with dirt,
turning back a crinkled leaf to the hidden chinquapins. Once I lay
by the creek, birds conversing around me in familiar grammars.
Ahead military jets on dawn patrol are drawing criss-cross diagrams,
a hangman's game in pink pastel pencil on the light-blue sky.

Eating Alone

This is a strange way to live, in two or three places
at once, and where I am, no one knows that but me.
So even standing in line at the grocery is a comfort,
and before that, rolling the cart up and down the aisles.
Because at least I'm with other people, foraging for food
in the orchard, the field rows, the shelves stacked up with
merchandise. In line I see how the woman in front of me
has gathered her supper, ground hamburger, white bread.
I don't want that food. I just want someone to turn around—

Talk to me.

How can it be that we are all going to carry our plastic bags
out the snapping doors, and get in our cars, and leave each other,
drive away to eat in twos or threes or one alone, me in a blue room
with a map of India to study, a novel open next to three sunflowers
in blue plastic bottles on the table, Sunday night, and eating alone
with no one to talk to about fiction and truth, what exists and how.

I know that before my story there are all the other stories.
Whatever place I come to, one of you has been there before.

Writing Poetry in a Rented Kitchen

Late at night silence settles down around me,
then comes the big tick of the electric clock,
then a whispered click like a syncopated
second hand, insistent phrase that stops,
starts, repeats again, finger tap I follow,
broken thread of sound, to the window.

A thumb-sized green lace-winged creature
staggers back and forth on the wire mesh,
marching with its flick and tiny flam of noise,
what I'll hear as I lie down in my strange bed,
a little bic pen in a nervous hand clicking
and writing down words I'll read in my sleep.

A Temporary Job

Leaving again. If I didn't care, I wouldn't be
grieving. The particulars of place lodged in me,
like this room I lived in for eleven days,
how I learned the way the sun laid its palm
over the side window in the morning, heavy
light, how I'll never be held in that hand again.

Beating the Heat

That morning the heat wave tossed me up
into an ice-floe air-conditioned coffee shop.
Four dollars eleven cents got me food, a table.
At the cash register, a man pays and holds up
a receipt: *A prize—I've got to win—thousands!*
A woman frowns, hand under chin: *In up to
here.* A swimming pool, a flood, bankruptcy?
Next to me there's a man, his left ear crusted
with blood, plugged, white-bandaged, he sits
with nothing but a gutted muffin skin, proof
he could purchase enough to get off the street.
Under my hand, the newspaper gives advice:
Beat the heat! To those stuck at home: *Damp
washcloths on your head!* Read between
the lines for people thrown into the page's gutter,
like the Chicago heat wave, summer 1995,
seven-hundred-sixty-nine people trapped, baked
in their apartments until dead. Nothing done:
the landlords, the state shut those oven doors.
Who's eating who here? The fresh crusty loaves
splayed out in the display case. What of the person
who says, *Enough,* and decides to smash the glass?
Brecht sang: *Who is the bigger criminal—
the one who robs the bank or the banker?*
The bloody ear stares at us and waits for our answer.

Driving the Bus after the Anti-War March

We had a different driver on the way home. I sat
on the seat behind her, folded, feet up like a baby,
curled like a silent tongue in the dark jaw of the bus
until she flung us through a sharp curve and I fell.
Then we talked, looking straight ahead, the road
like a blackboard, one chalk line down the middle.
She said, nah, she didn't need a break, she was good
to the end. Eighteen hours back to home when
she was done, though. Fayetteville, North Carolina,
a long ways from here. The math of a mileage marker
glowed green. Was Niagara Falls near Buffalo? She'd
like to take her little girl some day, too little now, won't
remember. The driver speaks her daughter's name,
and the syllables ring like bells. I say I lived in her town
once, after another war. The boys we knew came home
men cocked like guns, sometimes they blasted and
blew their own heads off, sometimes a woman's face.
Like last summer in Fort Bragg, all those women dead.
She says, *One was my best friend.* Husband shot her
front of the children, boy and girl, six and eight. She calls
them every day, no matter where she is. They get very
upset if she doesn't call. Her voice breaks, her hands
correct the wheel, the bus pushes forward, erasing nothing.
There was a blue peace banner from her town today,
and we said stop the war, jobs instead, no more rich
men's factories, refineries, futures built on our broke bodies.
She said she couldn't go to the grave for a long time,
but she had some things to get right between them so
she stood there and spoke what was on her mind. Now
she takes the children to the grave, the little boy
he wants to go every week. She lightly touches and
turns the big steering wheel. Her hands spin
its huge circumference a few degrees here, then
there. She whirls it all the way around when she
needs to. Later I hear the crinkle of cellophane. She
is eating some peppermint candies to stay awake.

Riding the Trailways into the City

Two hundred miles out I get on and begin the long slide
through winter to the city, down the old watercourses.
Every half-hour a little glow of light lifts on the horizon,
vanishing as we take that exit and more of us climb on.
We pass the closed mills, crouched and sleeping, the barns,
boards falling, flesh off bones. We gather speed like a dart
to the center, knife to the heart, toward what we are always
leaving. Inside a few lights mark a kind of home where people
are reading or talking. We jostle hip to elbow with kin, people
we'll never see again, we who have been tossed up, out, behind,
after the giant combine of Capital threshed over the land.
We rustle and sway, and fast-food wrappers whisper in the aisle,
no while, no where, some of us hoping there'll be a job when
we get there, some of us already gone to where the work is,
all of us twisting in the tunnel's helical bore, funneled into
the city terminal, where we step down in the white light of next,
into thousands like us, massed, displaced, looking, sitting
head in hands with a child beside, yelling, as we are watched
from the security cage hanging overhead, TV monitors, huge eyes
blinking as thousands of us almost overrun Port Authority.

Playing the Guitar Underground

The man with the guitar sings *mi pobre corazón,*
his heart and an empty hat at his feet as he sings
on the island between the local and the express train.
On the way north, past the muscled mudflat river,
there was some shelter on the border that's not a border.
The bridge by the rattling cottonwoods, or a boxcar
near the *barelas* in Albuquerque, like the one where
he was born, one of eleven, five did not survive.
El perdito niño, his infant's white gown pinned
with tiny *milagros,* the bent leg, the pierced heart,
the double eyes that see forward and backward,
the house, the helping hand, the note that says,
Living on the street for so long and I am tired
and always hungry and sick, please help. A picture,
the three of them: *Venimos desde muy lejos.* Boxcars
head due east between watermelon-red and apple-red
mountains, New Mexico-South Carolina. But when
he comes to the green valley there is only one apple
after another in his hand, bleeding heart of Jesus,
take it and eat. Like the red rose he holds, standing
all day at the entrance to the highway tunnel under-
ground. He'll trade his red for your silver, what's left
of the twists of fish and snakes and quetzal-tailed birds,
the silver that flew away from there to here over the Gulf,
or what's left of wages sent north from the *maquiladoras.*
He says that's NAFTA, *el tratado de libre comercio,*
that's how anyone without someone in the U.S. starves
or leaves the village to follow money that's free to move.

In the broad-brimmed bowl of the hat, coins pile up
like grain, something to send home to replace the corn
that no one can afford to grow now in Michoacán.

Breakfast Again

Two children sit down beside me, and the table tilts
my hot milky tea. The older unfolds crisp bakery paper
for the younger. Outside, their father smokes a cigarette
in the doorway. They watch him through the plate-glass
window, they stare at him as their hands lift the food.

Breakfast is a dark-glazed sun on a white paper napkin,
or the dark side of the moon, moon-cake emblazoned
with a sign, twinned glyphs, perhaps happiness, health,
luck doubled. Two people support each other, pillars,
clasped hands, an archway over an unknown future.
Or push each other back, arm's length, locked opposites.

After breakfast I walk two blocks to the courthouse.
Inside people sit on the floor, backs to the wall, heads
down on knees, waiting. The hall smells like pee, piss
from the open toilets. I stand in a knot of others there
to get sentenced, back after a night and day in jail.
After the demonstration, after the undercover cop swept
my feet out from under, after the too-tight plastic cuffs,
after they separated the men and women as if they knew,
after they ran their hands inside our bras and panties, as we
stood in the hall for arraignment, the policewoman said:
Form a line. Back to the wall. Said: *Get back. Shut up.*
Said: *Listen to what I say.* We listened to five minutes of this.
Then one of us said: *If you'd talked that much to Mr. Diallo*
before you drew your guns, he would be alive today.

By then we'd missed breakfast, 4 a.m. cornflakes, milk.
Lunch at 10 a.m. was two pieces white bread, baloney,
a packet of mayonnaise, another pint of milk. The same
at supper so we asked for juice, and they said: *None.*

Then a prisoner got sent in with a cardboard box, sudden
oranges, whispered advice as he tossed the bright fruit:
Got to speak up for yourself in here. Then the cell door shut.

Parallel bars, our iron gate to freedom, the xylophone of fate.
For some, the future welded over with a metal grate.

Hooking Up the Power

The yellow crane lowers its neck, its beak, its hook.
A man on the ground talks to a man at the gears, his hands
finger swizzle *up,* finger swizzle *down,* horned fist, thumbs
touch, *in, closer,* thumbs and fingers yap, yap, *let go, let go!*
He waves this way, that, casual, and the weight obeys.
He's signaling down a green metal box, it hovers, his hand
speaks to four men standing at the corners, they fasten
beaded wires into the invisible grid holding the flux, the pulse,
the electric water they switch on. The crane man lowers the box
over the last inch, careful as a glass of water set on the table.

The old crane operator says there were two, three hundred
workers in his building, production levels unbelievable, end of
the Korean War. He was pouring tons of steel over their heads,
no brakes, one lever vertical, one horizontal, got into a swing,
hit a skid of machines. *I almost killed a man.* Pure luck
the equipment fell like a tent over him. He climbed down,
threw his operator's badge on the floor. That's how the foreman
knew he'd quit, middle of the shift, so loud he couldn't hear,
couldn't talk. Except he could have gone anywhere in the world
where they were making steel, and made himself understood.

When he visited there not long ago, it was fields and grass,
seven or eight miles of buildings gone where once the smoke
profaned everything. When I pass by later, the men have gone.
They've left behind the blank box. One told me it's called a switch,
like on a wall. There's nothing else to show they hooked up power
enough for a parking garage, two high-rises either side. Light,
    spoken.

Teaching a Child to Talk

Next door a woman comes out, late afternoon, a child in her arms.
She speaks low, as if there's just the two of them. She says to him:
Listen to the little birdies, and he tilts his head and listens to
the common sparrows talking in the hedge. He listens as they argue
back and forth in their dialect of nature, as the street clatters, commuters
take a shortcut home. She says: *Listen.* And he turns his head to follow
the fugitive motion, the small streaked wings opening and folding,
the relentless chirp from a tiny blunt beak, the sound almost
     within reach.

Shoveling Sand

7 a.m., just light, and someone is already shoveling sand
at the construction site. A Black man leans forward, braced,
sneakers buried in the damp pile. He shifts to get his balance.
He knifes the blade in and pries up weight, straining for
a second, the pan low, like one arm of the scales of justice.
Then he flings the load up onto the screen sieve of the hopper
where it falls into finer grains. Mixed with cement and water,
it's already mortared in bricks three stories high, north and east
walls up, shelter for the white workers finishing inside.

Outside, he digs, and separates seashells, stones, from the sand.
The steady irregular beat of his shovel strikes like waves coming in,
high tide that crumbles and collapses a few inches of land, or as if
by the grave a hand gathers dirt from the edge and throws it in.

Picketing the Bargain Store

They say: *We do not lack imagination.* They watch
the boss try to harness them with word, threat, and trick.
They know he is out front getting photographed under
the red-white-and-blue Grand Opening banner, there
to remind shoppers of a national holiday, a victor's war.
They know they are inside fourteen hours a day, seven
days a week, once three days straight, no break,
one pizza a day to eat. Inside, they bend, grasp, lift
up onto the shelves the stuff for someone else's house,
bottles of bleach, welcome mats, thin pastel towels,
the green-and-gold peacock porcelain clocks,
each crowned head arched back to look at how well
it carries time in its belly. They make $2.74 an hour,
no benefits, no overtime. At night they sleep on the floor
of someone else's 99 Cent Dream Bargain Store.
They are here today to say: *¡Basta! Not us, not any more.*

Five workers say: *Enough.* Not enough yet for the police to lift
the blue barricades off the truck and set them to guard the store.

Passing Food Up and Down the Table

At dinner after the conference, she says, no, she doesn't like her job,
she liked working at the auto plant better. Though she put the window
units in backwards, at first. Mid-size cars. She laughs, a grimace: *Yeah,
the auto plant. After that, food prep at the cannery.* Now home health.
Like any job it's got its pros and cons. Like management trying to fire her.
The anti-war work, they can't stand it. But the flexibility is good. She
doesn't talk to us about her clients, about the going into an old person's
apartment, the sitting down by her on the crumpled bed, saying, *What do
you need? What can I get for you?* No, she says, she doesn't like the job at
all, but she gets to do exactly what they want to fire her for, the phone calls,
the press releases. *End death for corporate profit, end utility shutoffs. End
the fires.* In small closed rooms the kerosene fumes and blazes, fire eats up
the air, the furniture, a fuse of hair. She does what she needs to, daytime,
and writes up the work reports late at night. No, she's not worried about
losing the job, you can't worry about things like that, there's too much to do.
We are passing food up and down the table, twenty of us, szechuan bean curd,
noodles, and steamed salmon with rice. She says, *This fish gave its life for us,
the least we can do is eat every bit,* forking over the fretwork of bone,
and opening her mouth to taste the last shred of tattered flesh.

Demanding Water

I didn't know when the deluge came. I was in bed up north
where the rain that fell all night pattered about its safe routine,
making a bigger room for me to sleep in. But the levees broke
in New Orleans. People hacked through the ceiling to the roof
if they had an axe. If they didn't, they drowned standing up.
Who knows how many died, mostly Black women and children,
the poor, the old. The government saw it coming. Every summer,
ten times or more, the giant arms will uncurl and start to spin
as weather men guess which city might be hit. They call it Mother
Nature—No. My mother could plan. So I call it a government
unfit to rule, no longer compatible with you and me, *incompetent
to assure an existence* to those trapped inside its earthenware dam,
the river on one side, the lake on the other, the muddy-fingered
water pulling down an ill-built foundation, cracking the concrete
poured on top of flimsy sheet metal while the stop-gap money
is dropped in bombs on Baghdad, blasting open a street corner
where broken pipelines gush not oil, but water into dusty gutters.

The people stand by their dead and look at us. They demand: *Where
is the food? When will we have water?* The radio offers
more tragedy and says the government has a plan. Yes, there is
a plan. But it's not ours. The problem is, the plan is not ours.

Ants, Massing

Today I made a foray to where the ants
massed yesterday, crumbs of dirt seething
like magma through the cracked walk, volcanic.
But today, around the corner, back and forth—
there's nothing left, not a speck, just a flick
of white rump flying away, discreet predator.

This is not a pixellated 'toon about workers
as made by Disney—the smiling version of us
with six legs and big chomping mandibles,
animated antennae, anti-communist. No.
I had thirty minutes before work, I walked
to see the ants. Maybe they got eaten up.
Maybe they stuck together with pheromones,
memory, communication, and got safely gone.
The sidewalk's been swept clear by someone,
and what's left is the story I'm telling you here.

IF WE
JUMP UP
NOW

Fighting Fire

The firefighter hated the Academy Awards. *Those tuxedoed*
actors just read a script. They hadn't saved a soul, not one.
They didn't build a damn thing. In his spare time he cut stained
glass, he made presents for his friends' promotions, they
didn't need another bottle of rum. He made transparent
landscapes, a red house beating like a bloody heart in the sun.

Like Ana who left animal parts on the sidewalk to see who would
notice, who dug her own grave and filled it with gunpowder
instead of her body, lit it, a silhouette of fire jumping up and out.

Jump up, jump up. Let the words leap out of our mouths,
let us follow ourselves out of the burning now, out of
the dying house, out from under the blood slowly dropping
onto our foreheads, onto our closed eyelids. Let's get up now.

Distribution

Eight hours in a box the size of a phone booth, she's
at the front of the shift as I drive through and says,
Listen to me, sweetheart, don't cry, holds the phone
with one hand, hands me change with the other, says,
Don't cry, can you listen to mommy for a minute?
No way to leave her island wedged between the cars
flowing up the Bayonne bridge, above the stacked orange
ocean containers, truck ziggurat, railway apartments,
everything inside them gone to cram shelves in stores
where outside a man dressed all in white, rouged lips,
veiled head, asks for change. Why can't he have a home?
Why can't the long-armed cranes of Newark lift him
one container next to Ikea, he could walk in and choose
a bed, a rug, an assemble-it-yourself chair, why not?
The longshore workers, hands on the levers, know all about
distribution of goods, just-in-time inventory, they've shut
the flow down more than once, their hands on the faucet,
said to big business, *We made it, you took it, give it back.*
Give it back. Yes, how do we get our lives back?

The steelworker said, *Vinnie tried to get me to write it*
down, but at the end of the day, I couldn't, every day
so hard, full of noise, the heat, the machinery, I felt, I felt
what was going on but—The prisoner said, *The sun that day*
was leaning left, the shadows leaning right where he tried
to climb across the razor wire, looked like they'd slaughtered
a hog where he dropped. Whoever gets the controls here—
the payphones, the laundry, the vending machines—*they've*
hit the jackpot—He, she, we said, *Oh, love, oh precious love,*
my mind is cruising—and J.B. Hunt and Roadway Express
have locked us out because we are the ones who know
how to get from California to Memphis, and to the back road

past the docks at sunset along the water, the cranes asleep
for the night, while the climbers, door-unlockers, thumb-
and-finger doers, the people who sat and thought high up
in the glass forehead during the day, have now gone home—

Past the ticket collector in the Turnpike booth, the woman at the end
of her shift, the woman who can raise, who can lower the barricades.

Standing in the Elevator

There's the awkward moment when the elevator doors close,
and we try not to breathe as loud as the big animals we are.
No words, because there's too much to say and nothing
for our hands to do except punch the up/down button again.
We don't need some fancy research to tell us how we want
to be together, standing over a table strewn with puzzle
pieces, lifting one jagged edge to fit against another,
me matching the piece of blue sky you just made. Sure, we're
in here because we need the money but it's not even survival
by itself. Like the day the power failed, some of us stuck
in the elevator, and the building burning from the top down.
The cleaning guy had just his bucket and a squeegee blade.
He jimmied the doors open, he forced the steel doors apart,
in the vague light from the windows five people could see
enough to find their way out. Now that I'm back at work,
and some guy at a stoplight asks to squeegee my windshield
for a dollar, I think of that. Jobless, I thought I'd never hear
our niagara of sound going up the stairs again, never step,
immersed, into tens of thousands rushing to work. One molecule
in the many, carried along toward the purpose of our day.
It's never really about the money, except for the guys at the top.
They know how to make money off of us. We know
how to make things with each other. That's what we want to do.

Flight

I am interrupted by the flight attendant, who asks me about my laptop, and then about my writing. She's just trying to stay awake, talking to me to stay up for the rest of her trip, She says, *It's the same for us as for you. The delay,* and wondering if we'll get where we're going. She wonders whether she'll get back to Houston, not really home, but home now, where she sleeps, but also home is California, where she pays bills. She says she doesn't have a home. *Homeless, I guess,* she says, laughing ruefully. She keeps track of where she is at any moment in any day by her "cheat sheet," a folded and refolded printout of her flights for the week, hanging in a plastic badge holder around her neck. Six legs is a bad day, because there's not enough time to get off the plane and get something to eat. She's had this job for two years, is halfway up the seniority roster. People don't like the work, they quit, they get fired, they want to start a family. Jet lag? She just tries to stay awake. I imagine her as a clock with the hands spinning crazily, like in a Charlie Chaplin movie, the madness of working in a sky factory. Her passengers inch through the security lines toward her, past the police and their dogs at Departures, past Army reservists with rifles at the ready behind the x-ray machines. We take off our earrings and watches, our coats, our shoes. We stand there barefoot. We take off our belts and we hold our pants up with one hand. From time to time, they take some of us away into a corner, behind a screen, behind a door, if our name is on the list. Everyone behind the machine has the list, and no one will say where it comes from.

The New Commuter War

The snow falls up here! she says. White moths
sputtering up, and black crows storming down
past the porch windows. We're not up so high,
enough to see over the twilit valley, how night
lights blink like computer red LEDS. How high
up do you have to be to see what's happening?

The eye is not enough. Media moguls hand us
plastic 3-D glasses to look at earth wars moved
to another planet, they turn some people blue,
and burn beauty into mesmerizing ashes to drift
onto our hands as we sit in the theatre, front row,
perhaps next to a soldier living secret in this city.

Mornings he commutes to war to fly a death-reaper
unmanned drone, someone, the U.S. Army says,
just doing a job. That's a lie. He's making nothing.
Jerking a joystick, trained in games of conquest,
he kills a target on the screen, and at day's end
he drives home to his children, while in a valley
he's never seen or been to, ashes fall like snow

on a shattered house, on a dozen people dead,
on the blood and guts of the ugly, rotting truth.

Tegucigalpa

Silver hills of clouds, sullen light in the east,
an eyelid of cloud closed over the sun. No going
back, this porch for a garden that used to be,
a narrow ledge, a few pots, spearmint, lavender,
the mornings I knelt to weed, uptorn stinging,
shadow dew on my cheek, hands clotted with red
clay, the place gone forever, the house bulldozed,
a three-foot sweetgum tree rooting in the garden.
.

At the house below, a goodbye, a man steps
out of a doorway a few steps, looks back, the door
already closing. At the street he looks back again.
The door is still closed. From here I see the roads
flow out through the south valley where the clouds
gather and sit and wait at the grey-blue ridges.

Behind me the TV news flickers but has no news
that tear-gas boils in the streets of Tegucigalpa.
A friend sends: *Revolutionary situation developing.*

The sun blinks orange and dark red leaves serrated
at the edge of horizon. Tearing open what is today
to see what is inside, digging underneath, grasping
the edge that turns in our hands from knowing to act.

Sparks Fly Upward

On the way to work, I'm given a ratchety
static of rain hitting cement and the roadway.
Going home, against the dark screen of sky,
I see the trees blazing up in their dying,
their fallen leaves making a carpet of sparks.
If I could jump into their bonfire! If I
could fall headlong into that brief glory.
Dying and coming back is what trees
promise us—coming back as ourselves,
arms spread, the sun pulling life up
through our veins, so we play a new song
on our xylem xylophone. But, drinking
coffee at Sparky's, I read that the newspaper
Reverend Graham says reincarnation is not
the answer. No—evolution is. I don't fear
my imperfections or punishment after death.
It's that I don't want to be done with this joy,
matter striking consciousness, making
the thoughts and words that fly out to find
you. How we yearn to stay alive long enough
to find out what happens next. We burn to do
even as time's conflagration is consuming us.
The walk is littered with red leaves scorched
with brown, still veined with green. That's us,
scattered on the ground for who comes next.

Arwhoolie

The shift from grey to blue, the clouds askew,
slowly giving us the sun, and taking it back again,
each huge presence flirting with humidity. Weather
like home, far south, the laundry on the line
hanging heavy and wet. How many days to dry
that here? How much sweat? On the farm, a man
could find his clothes in dawn dark by his smell.
On Sunday down the hill, a gospel band yells
the old arwhoolie call from the field: *I'm coming.*
I'm not tired. East sun over my shoulder as I walk.
The clouds move their light weight without thought.
Yet we are tired. To keep going we call out loud.
Now I make that sound here on paper, the unworded vowel
deep, climbing up out of grief into the mouth, naked work.

A Pile of Dirt at the Museum

The people stand in the photograph, in a basement or in an underground
parking lot, their arms upraised, palms flat up to hold up the weight
pushing down on them. They are the pillars, the foundation,
     the unseen
holding up all that is visible. In the next room, a great wall unscrolls,
nothing but digital bricks, ceiling to floor. All that hauling flattened
to almost nothing, except for a pile of dirt, pure art, untouched, waiting
there for us to bury ourselves, so tired, so tired, at the end of work.

The museum guard says they dug that dirt up from somewhere, maybe
around here, and the maintenance guys, they'll be here on the last day,
fighting to get it for their gardens. We are all fighting for something.
As for me, turn me back into dirt when I die. Put me in the furnace,
and that little pile of bone and mineral—throw me onto the garden,
or pour and mortar me between the bricks to make a new foundation
for a world where we will have more to say of a person on their last day
than that she worked for her whole life and then she died.

Opening the Book on Tomorrow

John Finlay died the week after our call, his mother said,
as if he'd just been waiting for one last jangled hail
from the land of the living, and then he began to fail,
eyesight darkening to his childhood behind the lids,
specks of fireflies, or the star-flecked river we fell
laughing into that night our boat began to sink. He lay
in his room in his mother's house, other end of the road,
where it comes from, white sand, red dirt, before it goes
on to asphalt and street lights. And if he were alive now,
with plenty of medicine, would he say the epidemic's
over? Maybe he'd say his life was like a house fallen in
on its foundation, kudzu covers it, no one remembers.
The place he was fills with time like water, time
scouring him away, until this is what I have left:

The memory of how he stood to say good-bye the night
he held my newborn, petting the mewling baby, his floor
strewn with student papers, him pacing under the bare light,
him next to the digital postcard of Sarah Okiri in Harare,
her neighborhood where a fourth of the teachers will not live
to the next generation of children, no opening the book
on *tomorrow and tomorrow and tomorrow,* no school at all
for Sarah Okiri, ten years old, in her flip-flops and blue
sweatshirt and skirt, first-born who stands with one sister
by the hand and holds the smallest, has since her father
died and then her mother. She says, *It's not too late.*

She doesn't mean cost-benefit analysis, Anglo-American
conglomerate chief executives watching miners' bodies piled
on one side of the scales, the price of gold rising on the other.
Safety isn't Pentagon bases in Dijbouti, she doesn't get cash
from Chevron oil spilled in the Niger or its burning flares of gas.

It's not too late, says Sarah, and the others who dance protest
in the streets or give the open-palm blow, shouting, *No, no, no!*
hearing more than one last voice or words from another shore
before the falling roar when their bodies finally carry them away.

Answering the Automated Voice

No poetry done since that last phone call,
the corporate pharmacy, the automated voice:
You are denied. We cancel. Wanting to stamp
something into oblivion, but there's nothing
to kick. At night your fever jumps, you are up,
I roll over into sheets soaked with your sweat.
What furnace of words would be enough, what
could hold this loss that stands closer than you,
your dear body, and me. Wanting to kill what
is killing you. Yes, there is disease, but yes,
there is profit. The all-day-news about health
never says the system needs us sick to death
or else there would be no profit. My hours
on the phone trying to reach another human
being, then they read the regulations and say:
No. But do they have someone sick at home?

We only got when we fought, aiming higher
up, one word after another loaded like a gun.

The Street of Broken Dreams

The dog lunged at me and choked on its chain
guarding a house on the street of broken dreams.
What does it take to be safe? A sun-porch window
barred shut with a wood-spooled bed frame. Fradon
lock store down the block, a giant curlicue key
advertising sleep all night, sweet dreams. A bumble-
bee in the clover fumbling to find its damp-dirt home.

No way to tell who owns my neighborhood homes
until the for-sale-by-bank signs grow overnight,
and of course there's the bank at James and Lodi
with the blue light, CHASE, that stays on 24/7.
On my street some people harrow a vacant lot,
green turned under into small rows, they harvest
weathered rocks and pile those up in the corner.
In another city, some foreclosed people got so angry
the big finance company had to hide its sign, AIG.
The people were so angry. That makes me feel more
safe, the people come out of their houses to shout:

We demand. Not rabble and rabid, not shadow, not terror,
the neighbors stand and say: *The world is ours, ours, ours.*

The Dow Turns Red

At the mini-mart: *"Major Bank Fails in the South."*
Wall Street quivers. This street not so far north.
Some three or four Black men under a sycamore
or seated in the sun, talking each other through.
The lopsided houses, the cracked glass windows
waiting to swallow the last narrow icing of cold.
The jobs went south, further south, Wall Street
moving money around the world for profit, the sun
never sets on capital gain. What does that mean?
People somewhere else paid less to work more,
one day they're out of work under noon's glare, or
another man I pass, doing car repairs on the street:
Trying to make a living. What can I say? *Me too.*
I'm wondering how long my job will last, a place
to go every day, a shade, a shape we live inside
even as giant invisible hands hold and squeeze,
even as they fail and fall open. The Dow turns red
in the wreck, but the color of our blood isn't money.

The Wednesday after May Day:
Η προσπάθεια συνεχίζεται

A tanager flew its black-winged red flag in a thicket.
I stood watching in the rain, waiting for its whistle.

The radio had announced finance ministers to consult,
sounded quite deliberate. But the TV split realities:
To the right, a money trader, hands over eyes, hid
from the crevice of loss his numbers were falling into.
To the left, a sound I'd never heard, a fiery whoosh
like a furnace, some kind of engine pounding, unison
rhythm, a crowd in Athens chanting to advance,
retreat, advance against a thin grey fence of police,
their barbed arms. The people outnumber the police,
they raise fists again, again, to break down that fence.

The world watches the line bend, the people create
a rift, the numbers shift, the people shout, *No, no,*
they won't work until they die so the banks can live,
make corporations into corpses is their cry—*Make!*

On the asphalt blackened by rain, green-winged
maple seeds scatter the same small mathematical
symbol: the angle reads less than < or greater than >

Repeated by the millions, the meaning depends on
where the people stand and what they mean by *equal.*

The Great Leafing-Out

The man with the rattlesnake coiled on his chest
yells in my face, the battleships loom battlements
above us, and the crowd clanks over a gang plank
to hear the fulminating speaker throw his words.
They say they're not racist, they say they don't hate.
We say words won't make it so, better show us,
as we hold our placards as shields against
three hundred of them, thirteen of us, that's why
we are here, chanting, *Fight, fight, fight,* the slant
slice of our hands, our signs, hold a patch of grass
for us to root stubbornly there, a pole of ideas:
Corporate greed breeds racism. A job is a right.
Now three men shout at the perimeter, *Get a job!*
as if to battle them about the future isn't work.

An hour later we're at a Thruway rest stop, fast
food, faster cars, we eat at seventy miles an hour,
no sign anything has happened, except a thin
digital proliferation of messages, interruptions,
interpolations, a small line in Boston is snaking
through the bigots. The struggle for the present
moment from which the future comes, shouting.

Yesterday the maple tree dropped its own reality
at my feet, a twig waving red-green paws, curled
with little finger muscles of seed. Over my head
and further than I can see, the tree tops brighten
in a green sunrise. The beautiful moment between,
when something has begun and is not finished yet.

Burning Water

In the YouTube video a man flips a lighter, flare,
holds it to a belching faucet, the water catches fire,
not a miracle, the companies hydro-fracking the earth
for gas, the movement of Capital in ground water—

And there's that unpoetic word again, so overt,
admittedly abstract, some even say clichéd, a word
I'd never even heard when me and the cousins sat
in the shrimp boat stern, grownups on vacation
playing penny poker all night in the front, as we
watched the dark horizon line between deep sea
and deeper sky fall behind us and never change.

We hung our legs into strange bioluminescent foam
flung up by our wake, if we'd scooped the water
up with a glass jar as we did the air for fireflies,
we'd have caught eighty species, galactic diatoms
invisible to our eye, to us just some murky water
from the Gulf, which is licked over today with oil
from the blown-out rig, all for lack of a cut-off
trigger, costs half a million, comes out of the foul
profit now crawling on sand—or the drill was too fast,
after all time is money, that is, less for the workers,
more for the company, yes, theory again—or pooled
experience, since there is a connection from abstract
to specific, the translucent organisms that work
to filter water are this morning drinking in oil,
when they float to the surface, when the sun stares
down on them long enough, they will begin to burn
from inside out, microscopic dying stars in the Gulf.
But not the result of a natural, inevitable process.

What I mean is once I saw a flock of little sting-rays,
each no bigger than my palm, arrowing like tiny geese

where water met sand in the shallows of Tampa Bay,
I stood in the Gulf and they winged between my feet,
going somewhere I didn't know. Now what will they eat?

The connection between there and now not inevitable,
matter striking our minds, us trying to catch the spark,
consciousness.

If We Jump Up

Let new words leap out of our mouths.
Let our hands be astonished at what we have made, and glad.
Let us follow ourselves into a present not ruled by the past.
If we jump up now, our far will be near.

NOTES

"The only danger is not going far enough": Muriel Rukeyser,
   The Life of Poetry (New York: A.A. Wyn,1949), 201.

Opening the Mail: For Kriste Grubbs, records assistant.

Making Art: For Tom Duncan, sculptor and painter.

Giving a Manicure: P'ansori is a Korean folk narrative or epic,
   chanted, recited and performed to a drum beat. Choi Don Mee
   and Yi Yon-ju are contemporary Korean feminist poets.

Farming in the City: In memoriam, Susan Atefat Peckham, poet.
   A *genena* is a small garden attached to a house.

A Small Business: For Vidya Maharaj, who also explained that
   Holi is the first day of spring in Hindu tradition, celebrated
   by Trinidadians of East Indian heritage.

Ordering Paperclips: For Rebeca Toledo, who said *"Fear...."*

Forgetting to Clock Out: For Beverly Slack Hiestand, nurse educator
   and retired chief steward, CWA Local 1168.

Collecting Social Security: In memoriam, Thelma Brown, clerk.

Retirement: In memoriam, Virginia Earl Brown Pratt, social worker.

Playing the Guitar Underground: With homage to the art of Ruben
   Trejo and Ray Martin Abeyta.

Breakfast Again: In 1999, Amadou Diallo, an emigrant to the U.S.
   from Liberia, was killed by four New York City policemen who
   fired 41 shots at him as he stood unarmed in the door of his
   apartment. More than 1700 people were subsequently
   arrested in mass protests against police brutality in the city.

Hooking Up the Power: For Milt Neidenberg, steelworker and union
   organizer, and Rosie Neidenberg, who said *"profaned."*

Demanding Water: Italics are taken from the *Communist Manifesto.*

Fighting Fire: In memoriam, Ana Mendieta, performance artist.

Distribution: With acknowledgement to the work and poetry of
   men imprisoned at the Foothills "Correctional Institution,"
   Morganton, North Carolina.

Tegucigalpa: In 2009, in their capital city, thousands of Hondurans protested the U.S.-backed right-wing coup against left-leaning elected President Manuel Zelaya.

Opening the Book on Tomorrow: In memoriam, John Finlay, poet. The story of Sarah Okiri is from her 2001 narrative, sent to Africa Alive! for its "Postcards from Africa" web initiative, about her experience as a 10-year-old Kenyan girl living in the AIDS epidemic.

The Wednesday after May Day: Η προσπάθεια συνεχίζεται translates as "The struggle continues."

ACKNOWLEDGEMENTS

A heartfelt thank you:

to my editor Andrea Selch, for her enthusiasm and work on this book

to Leslie Feinberg, for her loving support, editorial art, beautiful photographs, and political acumen

to Judith Arcana and Don Mee Choi, for their astute comments on these poems

to Raphael Campo, Alfred Corn, Mark Doty, Cornelius Eady, Charles Flowers, Rigoberto González, Ellis Guzman, Marilyn Hacker, Richard McCann, Hilda Raz, for their support in many different ways.

Earlier versions of some of these poems have been published
        in these periodicals:

5 AM, American Poetry Review, Arts & Letters, Bloom, Columbia Poetry Review, Feminist Studies, The Gay and Lesbian Review Worldwide, Gulf Coast, Meridian, New Labor Forum, On the Issues: A Progressive Women's Magazine, The Paterson Literary Review, Persimmon Tree, Ploughshares, The Progressive, Prairie Schooner, The Rambler, Rethinking Marxism, Smartish Pace, Stone Canoe, and *The William & Mary Review*

        and these anthologies:

Poets Against the War (Thunder's Mouth/Nation Books, 2003); *100 Poets Against the War* (Salt Press, 2003); P*ractice, Practice, Practice: ProLiteracy Worldwide* (New Readers Press, 2005); F*ire and Ink: An Anthology of Social Action Writing* (University of Arizona Press, 2009); *Love Rise Up* (Benu Press, 2010)

        and this blog:

Poets for Living Waters (www.poetsgulfcoast.wordpress.com).

"Chopping Peppers," "Getting Money at the ATM," "Giving a Manicure," " Playing the Lottery," "Reading the Classifieds," "Picketing the Bargain Store," "Shoveling Sand," "Breakfast," "Cutting Hair," "Picking Up a Job Application," "Teaching a Child to Talk" are from *The Dirt She Ate: Selected and New Poems* by Minnie Bruce Pratt © 2003. Reprinted by permission of the University of Pittsburgh Press.

Special thanks to **belladonna*** and Rachel Levitzsky who published some of these poems as chapbook #46 in their series.

A New Jersey State Council on the Arts grant helped support the writing of these poems.

The text of the book is typeset in 10-point Minion.
The book was designed by Lesley Landis Designs.